Going on an Airplane

A TODDLER PREP BOOK™

We're going on an airplane!

There will be so many new things to see and do. Let's talk about what we do at the airport and when we're on an airplane.

When we get to the airport, we take our bags from the car and walk inside.

Then we get in line at the ticket counter and wait patiently for our turn.

When we get to the front of the line, we drop off our bags and get our tickets to board the airplane.

Next, we go through security to make sure
everyone stays safe.

We send all our things through the X-ray machine and walk slowly through the scanner.

After we go through security, we walk through the airport to find our gate.

A gate is where we sit and wait to get on the airplane.

We can read books or play games while we wait...

...or we can even watch airplanes land and take off!

When it's time to get on the airplane, we gather our things and get in line.

Then, we walk through a long tunnel called a jet bridge.

We made it to the airplane! There are a lot of seats inside. We walk down the aisle and find our seats.

Then, we sit down and wait patiently for others to board the airplane. Don't forget to buckle your seatbelt!

The flight attendant teaches us about safety and tells us when it's time to take off.

Hang on tight! Sometimes it's bumpy when we take off.

We can play games, eat snacks, read books, or take a nap while we sit in our seats.

And if we need to use the potty, there's even a bathroom on the airplane.

Sometimes, the flight attendant brings us a drink or a snack.

They also tell us when it's time to land.

Once our airplane lands safely on the ground, we get off and walk to baggage claim.

At baggage claim, we get our bags off of a long conveyor belt.

We did it! Now we
are ready to have fun.